Wise Guy

I

It all starts ... however then, where does anything begin? Back at the very first minutes of Creation, perhaps, or down in some long-ago tale, its significances and also purposes discolored now right into the darkening past. Every story's opening is a little arbitrary, one way or another. Every beginning is a small lie.

Still, considering that this particular tale worries a thief called Bart Sagan, we should probably begin where he did-- the mid-day of December 18, a week prior to Xmas, when he combated his way through the icy winds that cut down High Road to satisfy a pal at the Evergreen Pub and ask her for some aid. Hatch a fast plan with her, to put it simply. Story a little crime.

As Bart laid out the story for his pal, everything beginnings when a medication jogger for the neighborhood criminal offense lord Harry King obtains himself rattled-- rattled great as well as hard, convinced he's only half a jump ahead of the cops.

Billy is that jogger's name; Billy Euston. And maybe he's appropriate to assume the authorities are surrounding him. Or perhaps he's just gone bananas. That recognizes? Ultimately, all medicine joggers visualize they hear footsteps, sneaking along behind them, and start to shiver in their sleep. Yet in either case, there this scrawny, longhaired Billy character locates himself: abandoning his auto on a south-side street to duck down an alley, lugging an old brown-leather luggage.

Naturally, with twelve three-kilo plans of heroin inside, the traveling bag evaluates almost eighty extra pounds. Both hands on the deal with just to carry it, wheezing like an asthmatic sheep, also Billy, loopy as he is, begins to recognize he's not obtaining far. But up ahead, midway down the block, he sees a large delivery van appearing of an entrance. And it's then that Billy has the first of his brilliant ideas: He'll shake off the cops by slipping around the vehicle and also hiding in the delivery lawn.

Just trouble is, the yard's full of people: paper-baggers completing their lunches, and cigarette smokers taking a nicotine break, and also motorists standing around in little knots, screaming back and forth while they consume their coffee and wait on their loads. The place where he believed he might hole up for a while-- evade the authorities, possibly call Mr. Kin individuals for a pick-up-- becomes the filling dock of a huge shipping facility, a busy madhouse in the center of the Xmas rush.

It's not so much a strategy as large momentum, as Bart described it, that brings Billy ahead right into the building-- red faced and sweating, scrambled by the trend of workers: a scruffy kid in a natural leather coat that's almost a sign on his back reading Apprehension Me, I'm a Wrongdoer, transporting a life-sentence tons of uncut heroin as well as trying to claim he belongs there.

Inside, the delivery facility confirms also wilder. The last thing a paranoid, adrenaline-fueled medicine jogger requires is sound, and also this location is loud. Individuals yelling, forklifts banging about. An every-which-way tangle of conveyors-- you know the kind of thing: those waist-high tracks covered with little wheels to assist slide the packages along-- all clattering away. The structure resembles a hundred-decibel pinball device, as well as Billy's the sphere, jumping from bumper to bumper, tripping over people, stumbling right into boxes, trying to find a departure. He notifications a guard down the aisle providing him the fish-eye, possibly, and also speaking into a radio, so he reduces around a production line of workers packing up Christmas boxes for mailing and also slides with a door.

Sadly, what he's walked into ends up being a storage room, the shelves loaded with empty white present boxes, quite gold bows on the lids. As well as it exists that Billy has his second of his intense concepts. He takes down a dozen of the boxes, loads a bag of heroin in each, as well as piles them on a moving cart. Then he shucks his jacket as well as conceals it behind the door with the luggage. He places on a roaming blue apron, to match the workers he's seen, and also gets hold of a dusty clipboard to look a lot more main.

A deep breath, and he's ready to go-- other than, attempting to maneuver the cart out, he runs right into a square-built woman, as stationary as a linebacker, wearing a red manager's apron. "There you are," she claims, like she understands him, taking hold of the cart. "Where in the name of all that's divine have you been the last hour?" Billy tries to wrestle the cart far from her, but she's more powerful than he is, there's a pair of guard standing only 5 feet away, and she's screaming, "Susan, Bob, the remainder of you, right here are the last of them. C'mon, c'mon, individuals, the vehicle's waiting."

Susan as well as Bob-- what appears like the entire assembly-line crew of packers-- come adding, and prior to Billy can say a word, they've ordered the gift boxes and loaded them for shipping. The linebacker at a loss apron snatches the clipboard out of his hand, blazes at him, and marches off, yelling, "Below are the addresses. Allow's go, people. Relocate, relocate, relocate." The guard give him that thoughtful shrug males share when one of them has just been flattened by a female, and there we are: Billy watches open- mouthed and also powerless, gaping like a fish, while maybe $10 numerous Harry King's property goes drifting down the river of conveyor tracks, through a label scanner, as well as out the door as Christmas provides for God understands that.

He constantly intends to make it a tale, Liz McCally grumbled to herself as her good friend Bart paused his tale of misadventures to sip at the warm drink he 'd bought. That's his weakness. Bart's the most effective of us, perhaps: wise, careful, always planning ahead. Solid, as well, keeping that kind of whipcord strength of a cattle ranch hand who appears like he considers a hundred extra pounds, leaking damp, but can understand an unbroken steed in a mid-day.

Liz shivered a little, as she viewed him across the table in among the Evergreen's back booths, his long safecracker's fingers stirring his cider with a cinnamon stick. A thin, wiry man with a wipe of black hair, handsome in a hideous, Abraham Lincoln means, Bart might be anything. Make a huge rating and retire, leave all of us behind. Yet he desires it to indicate something: to have a form, reveal some objective. He requires to turn every little thing right into a story-- a fable, topped off with a tidy little moral-- and also ultimately that's going to obtain him eliminated.

She liked Bart, she understood. Trusted him, would work with him on any type of parts of a job she recognized. Possibly she was also in love with him, a little. Yet she wouldn't tell him that, would not get tangled up with him, because it would certainly injure excessive when the end they all knew was coming for him finally arrived, like a hearse pulling up to the door.

Swirling her own drink, examining his hands, Liz missed Bart's explanation of exactly how Billy the Silly Youngster got out of the shipping center and also reported back to Mr. King. Not that she respected some medication jogger she 'd never ever met-- or Harry King, as for that went. She would certainly been a scam artist in this community long enough to know the ropes: Any person that crossed Harry King wound up knee-deep in the sludge at the bottom of the river, as well as Liz really did not figure she could find out water-breathing fast sufficient to run away with the kingpin's medicines or cash, if she were fool sufficient to steal them. Yet aside from that, why should it matter? You didn't get into one of Mr. King's cribs, in the same way you really did not attempt armed robbery at a police headquarters. Or else, you were cost-free to handle any type of work you believed your luck as well as skill would bring you through.

" What's this reached finish with me? With you, with any one of us?" she required, while Bart looked off right into the range as though he were trying to see the end, see what it all indicated-- the Legend of Billy the Unlucky.

He looked back at Liz throughout the table, smiled that uneven smile of his, as well as responded to, "Yeah, well, that's the 2nd part of the story."

Ends up, a number of bruisers had picked up Bart that morning, delicately scooping him off the pathway like well-dressed garbage collectors just as he was leaving his house. Silence in the vehicle, they stayed, as they drove him along. Not a word in the lift as well as without words down the marbled corridor, escorting him in silence through the mahogany doors and into the well-known penthouse suite of Harry King-- Harry King, in all his pomp and glory.

King looks, as Bart explained him for Liz, like a pig farmer that's invested way too much time with his pets. Greedy little eyes, quick and dubious. The profundity of a person who knows exactly how to obtain what he desires, as well as the rashness of someone who desires much more of it. The huge, sausage-fingered hands of a guy that suches as to hold things and also squeeze.

" You think this?" King barks to the area loaded with people as Bart is carried within, the doors closing behind him. A sycophantic little male in a black fit flinches as King swings a flashing necklace past him to wave over his workdesk. "A half million dollars, that's what this little cockroach intends to bill me."

The medicine globe's undisputed leader tightens his eyes and also stares for a minute at the flow of silver and diamonds like starlight around his hand. "Still, it's a quite point, as well as the wife will like it," he states, in a quieter voice. "All right, I'll get it. Frank, take the roach outdoors and provide him a check." He goes down the necklace in a glob back into its velvet-covered situation as well as hands it to the male on his opposite. "Mike, put this with the other presents you're having wrapped. I'll give it to her at the party on the 24th, when all the bigwigs obtain their presents. The rest of you, obtain the heck out of right here. I wish to speak with this guy."

A slim, longhaired child-- cotton wads in his puffy nose and also contusions basing on his face-- starts to move gratefully from his chair as well as sign up with the exodus, till King jabs a fat finger at him and also complexities, "Not you, Billy boy. Oh, no, not you. You remain as well as have a little conversation with us."

As the space empties, King occurs to the front of the workdesk as well as leans his buttocks back versus it, swing Bart to a chair before him. "Sorry concerning that," he introduces in the friendly tone that, in Bart's experience, usually suggests someone will aim a gun at his head. "Christmas Eve Day-- is that exactly how you say it? It sounds wrong, somehow." He provides Bart a puzzled look, after that lets it go. "Anyway, the afternoon of the 24th, I'm throwing a reception for the mayor, the head of the museum, perhaps the D.A., a loads of the genuine powers in this town. 'Establishing reputable credentials,' my legal representatives call it."

He shifts against the desk and looks over Bart's head at guides like wallpaper on the racks at the rear of the area. "Amusing aspect of reputable individuals," he adds. "You can provide money-- you have to provide cash: whole lots as well as great deals of it, all peaceful as well as discreet, if you wish to purchase right into their respectable globe. Yet if you attempt to provide something sensible as a little goodwill gift, a watch or a car or something like that, they lean back all insulted and smell like a maiden auntie who's simply heard an unclean word."

He sneers, "What you can provide, though, is food. It's the social thing to do, the lawyers tell me: a little gift for the family to reveal your heart's in the best place. So that's what they're obtaining from Harry King for Christmas." He aims over at the opposite side of the space, and Bart spins around to research the lengthy table loaded with tins as well as bottles and also half-wrapped presents. "Delicacy, truffles, Japanese mushrooms, crap like that. Coffee at $ 600 an extra pound from Sumatra or some damn area. A $2,000 bottle of a glass of wine $ 10,000 a box, that's what these little house presents are costing me, and none of it worth the pot to piss it away in. However decent, yeah-- oh so decent."

After that Harry King shakes his head like a horse chasing off a fly. "I'm chatting way too much. You're an active guy, so allow's get down to company. This," he claims, waving his hand towards the child in the chair, "is

Billy Euston, as well as he's shed something that comes from me. He's my sister-in-law's nephew, and also I would certainly never listen to the end of it if he fell down a trip of stairways and also broke his neck.

So maybe Billy isn't going to pay as high as he should for yesterday's mistake-- at the very least, not if you can fix it for him. Take him with you when you go, and he'll provide you the information about where and also just how he mislaid my residential property."

Bart opens his mouth to ask why he needs any information at all, yet King stands up a finger once again. "Below's the point. I know all about you, Bart Sagan. I understand you're perhaps the slickest burglar in my town. My community. I understand you have actually got a little crew of friends as well as helpers that you 'd despise to see anything happen to. Little Liz McCally, for instance, as quite as a picture. Be a pity if she got hurt. The bartender down at the Evergreen that passes messages for you. All the remainder of you independents."

He sneers once again. "All the rest of you small-timers. I've allow you function, allow you tackle your company, for as well long. And now it's tax day, around the city, and your bill simply came due. Obtain my home back for me, as well as we'll call it also."

Searching behind himself for an envelope, he includes, "The authorities do not recognize anything yet, do not have an idea regarding what's taken place, and I want it kept in this way. That's why I'm using you, rather than my very own males, for this job. You have an online reputation for being quick and also silent, not making waves-- so discover my residential or commercial property, quick and quiet. What's today, December eighteenth? I want everything back before New Year's." After that he throws the envelope right into Bart's lap. "Right here's some money, a couple of thousand dollars, for expenses. As well as perhaps there'll be a little bonus offer, if you get it done right, with no one ever knowing. However that's all."

Harry King grins, an emperor checking the world he has. "It's tax day, Bart," he repeats, rolling the expression around in his mouth like he's tasting it for the first time and also choosing he suches as the flavor. "Tax day, as well as everybody almost everywhere is going to pay. Currently take Billy here with you as well as remove. I've obtained job to do."

So Bart rises from his chair as well as leaves the penthouse, trailed by the hangdog Billy, much as Harry King's bruisers had actually brought him: never having claimed a word.

II

By the time Cicely D'Angelo captured him in her house-- by the time he 'd danced with her to a scratchy old record on the phonograph and also kissed her white hair in the light of a Xmas tree at the record's end-- Bart already recognized the job was going wrong.

Not that it had not started well. The disadvantage that Liz went for the delivery facility, for instance, proved easy enough. A brown distribution uniform was sufficient to obtain her through the door, she told Bart as she handed him the mailing list at midday the next day, December nineteenth. After that it was simply an issue of a little strategic bosom, a few tears welling up in her eyes, as well as a helpless-maiden tale of a lots messed up addresses that she was going to obtain terminated for, if she could not replace them. In by 9:00 that morning, out by 10:00, a printout of the checklist in her pocket.

" The individual who aided me, digging out the names as well as addresses from their computer system, is some type of nerd genius. Much better even than you, Bart, as well as I constantly thought you were the most effective. He'll end up running the location, if he can discover to maintain his paws on his key-board." Liz smiled indulgently. "He also found where the names came from-- the last entries in an advertising campaign from a couple of years ago. He was beginning to question why they were popping up again, all in the very same order, for a Xmas mailing this year, but I took care of to sidetrack him." She grinned again. "He's currently left me two messages, requesting for a day."

Bart examined the checklist for a minute or more prior to establishing it down on the pub table. He sighed, staring at his beverage as he mixed it with a slim pink- and-white swirled stick.

" What is it?" Liz asked.

" Hmm? Oh, this? It's warmed schnapps with a pepper mint candy walking stick," he answered. "I always order hot beverages in December. They taste like Christmas, in some way."

" No, you idiot," Liz snorted in exasperation. "Not the drink. The checklist.

Did you see the twist?"

Yes, Bart had seen it, like a boot to the head. 9 addresses in the city, 2 in the nearby residential areas. Or nearby sufficient, anyhow, that possibly he could complete the whole project in the days he had actually left before individuals began opening their Xmas presents. Burglarize eleven locations without leaving a mark, find packages, replace the heroin with something the exact same weight so the victims never understood they would certainly been struck, and after that elope once more hidden: not likely, yet at the very least conceivable. But the twelfth address-- that was difficult.

" Exactly how am I meant to obtain all the way bent on Minnesota as well as back in time to swipe the remainder of the plans?" he asked Liz. "For that matter, where do you mean it is-- this Moriah, Minnesota, place?"

" Up near the Canadian boundary," she addressed smugly. "Populace 2,412. Significant industries: wood and mining. Great deals of ice fishing. The neighborhood senior high school-- the Battling Beavers-- won the Minnesota Department II hockey event last winter and also are favored once again this year, if their goalkeeper gets over his mono in time. A few of the girls on the chat networks assume he caught it kissing that inexpensive, bottle-blonde supporter from International Falls, but they confess they do not recognize for certain. What are you looking at? I searched for the town online."

Bart giggled for the first time considering that Harry King had actually laid down his orders. "The trouble is," he clarified, "I do not know any type of great thieves out in the center of the nation. A person from below will have to go, and also it's practically difficult to obtain people for a severe out-of-town work this time of year. After the vacations, they're all broke as well as starving, yet before Xmas-- that's the one time they fret about being away from their households."

" I guess," claimed Liz slowly, "my relative can attempt, if you want. His name is Joey. Joey Jasper. He called a few days ago, looking for job. He's consistent, even if he is sort of a doob."

" A doob? Is that like a dweeb? "No ... "

" A geek? A half-wit?"

" C'mon, Bart. You understand what a doob is. It's a. a doob. It means-- oh, I do not understand. It means he's unfortunate, maybe. Like, if a work crumbles, you just know he'll be the one who obtains captured. However he will not steal from his partners, and how challenging can a town be? I indicate, we're talking Moriah, Minnesota, below. Not New York or Los

Angeles. The only worry is that they'll blunder the stuff for powdered sugar and utilize it to bake a cake for him."

He liked Liz, Bart knew: liked her nerve, liked her speed. Liked her looks, as well, he had to confess. Small, five-two or -three, perhaps, as well as overflowing with all-American cuteness-- a cuteness she relied on in far too many of her frauds, specifically that girl-in-distress regular she would work on anything also vaguely male. Yet her face: It meant something more.

Something getting to toward a private personality, an individual beauty. Her intense eyes, her hair ... He captured himself studying her as well as jerked his gaze back up towards the pub's front windows.

Unfortunately, Bart also knew that collaborating with Liz caused trouble.

She 'd gotten the lucky bounce so commonly, she would certainly concern believe that good luck ruled deep space, and it enticed her out in advance of herself-- rushing a job, shaking off the timing. Oh, she valued proficiency, also in somebody like the delivering company's computer man. Yet in the long run, she divided the globe into the fortunate as well as the unlucky, as well as she pressed too difficult. She's like a tennis gamer, Bart mirrored, without strategy other than to hurry the internet and take the sphere on the volley. You can win a great deal of points in this way, swipe a quick collection of games, however you tend to lose the long, dragged out suits, without ever fairly understanding why.

Bah, he believed, this company is making me sour. On any type of provided job, you relied on Liz wherefore she was efficient, as well as you maintained her out of the rest. And also why not? She was searching for her path, like everybody else. We're all stumbling about at night, seeking also the faintest glimmer in the sky to follow.

" How much does a kilo evaluate?" asked Liz, disturbing Bart's reverie. "A kilo-- what do you mean, just how much does it evaluate? It evaluates a kilo.

A kilogram."

" No, I imply just how much does it weigh in some regular weight? You understand, like a measure we normally use. The number of pounds?"

" Oh. Simply over 2 pounds. A kilo is 2.2 pounds."

" Okay," said Liz. "Currently we're cooking." She turned to look over her shoulder at the Evergreen's bartender. "Hey, Tim," she called out. "Just how much does a liquor bottle evaluate? Like a routine bottle of wine?"

" Full? 3, maybe four extra pounds," he addressed. "Depend upon how thick the glass of the container is."

" Thanks," she recalled. "So just how about that?" she turned once more to ask Bart. "Three kilos in each box, 2.2 pounds a kilo, that's 6.6 extra pounds. Call it six as well as a half. 2 bottles of red wine the ideal weight, as well as we have actually got what we require for the swap. No one's mosting likely to be too amazed by getting red wine for Christmas, right? No greater than stunned, anyway, than they are just by the fact that someone sent them an anonymous existing."

" Yeah, maybe," responded to Bart. "Visit the liquor shop, as well as see what you can locate. At the same time, I think I'll drive out to the suburban areas this afternoon. I've got to begin looking at these areas, figure out which ones are mosting likely to be hard to burglarize. See if I can assemble a plan."

"What else do you want me to do?"

" Nothing. Inform your cousin to call me right away, and also I'll fill him in, established him up with a plane ticket, obtain him moving. But or else, I want you out of it."

" I'm currently in it," Liz snapped. "Harry King put me there when he intimidated me as well as everybody else we understand. You can not shield us. Not from King. Not from any person."

" C'mon, Bart," she added, softening. "I understand you intend to be Santa Claus, bringing comfort as well as delight to all us bit wide-eyed children, impressed at exactly how smart as well as terrific you are. However also Santa has his reindeer and also those wacky fairies assisting him out. Let me call around, learn which of our pals remain in community, see if I can not speak one or two of them right into providing us a hand. A minimum of we can be good little elves as well as range out the addresses here in the city for you."

" No splitting in? No leaping ahead? Simply looking at them?" "Cross my heart," Liz swore, drawing an X on the front of her brown

uniform shirt, the look of innocence on her guileless face a better promise of dishonesty than anything Bart had actually seen in years.

Possibly Liz has it right, Bart was beginning to assume. No reluctance, no preparation. You simply walk in as well as attempt to make something take place. At least, that's the method it operated at the second home he went to examine. Using a dark green gas-company attire pulled from his trunk, he 'd driven gradually past the first of the country addresses-- developing, as ideal he could, a suggestion for just how to strike the tiny, green cottage.

The second address, nonetheless, ended up being up a long drive extending from a quiet suv street. The previous weeks of ice and snow, accumulated by the plows in long hedgerows, covered up the home boundaries, as well as before he totally realized he was on the estate, Bart had occurred the curve of the drive, in full sight of the front door.

An old-money sort of residence, it seemed, belonging as if by right in this old-money kind of suburban area. Maybe it had been a little ostentatious, back in the day, yet the mainstream of American architecture had long back flowed past it, and also the area currently looked nearly stodgy-- the pretensions of the subjected light beams, fancy stucco, as well as leaded home windows softened by the thick ivy gradually covering your home and the huge trees that had actually used the years to grow up around it.

Standing on the vast steps, her arms wrapped around herself for heat, was a lady in a gray outfit and also white sweater, suggesting vehemently in Spanish with a male in a parka, holding a shovel. The caretaker and also the groundskeeper, Bart presumed, with various concepts about what requires to be done. Not even the arrival of a complete stranger stopped their squabble, and also as he tipped from the vehicle to supply some spiel that could make up his existence, the lady simply eyed his attire and swung him around to the side of the large house where, probably, the gas meters were to be discovered.

Much as Bart disliked being seen by his targets, the possibility to check out the safety and security system was as well excellent to pass up-- as well as the opportunity confirmed even better than he had actually supposed. A window at eye level, in what resembled a kitchen. Noticeable through the window, a white Christmas box with a gold bow on the top, sitting in a nest of packaging product on the counter next to heaps of arranged mail. And also a couple of feet to the right, a side door opening right into a deserted cooking area. Unlocked, as well, he discovered when he gave the take care of an exploratory turn.

Now, consider that: an open door in what seemed like an empty house. It's hard to claim what even more of a welcome sign a burglar could desire in this life. A couple of fast actions down the hall, the bag of heroin lifted out of its box, some jars of expensive foods off the cupboard shelves placed inside to give a harsh suit of the weight, and the cover set carefully back on. Out once again with the side door, the tape-reinforced plastic bag held against his side. A ducked head and a wave at the still-arguing couple, and Bart had actually effectively finished the very first of the tasks Harry King had required of him.

He smiled as he paused his auto at the end of the drive to tuck the heroin under the traveler's seat and also look once more at the shipping listing. The twelve criminal offenses of Christmas-- currently eleven, he noted with contentment, erasing the name and also address of one Michael Stuyvesant: the victim of a smash and grab so lightning quick and also honey smooth that, with any kind of good luck, he would certainly never ever even know he would certainly been smashed and grabbed.

Hubris was the term Bart later on utilized to explain it: the self-confidence he felt after the Stuyvesant work, the feeling of invincibility that led him to drive directly back to the very first of the suv addresses-- the little green bungalow with the drooping eaves that belonged, according to the delivery list, to a woman named Cicely D'Angelo-- and also try his good luck at a 2nd daylight felony.

Naturally, because the individual to whom he at some point told the tale was the battered drug-runner Billy Euston, that wouldn't understand the word hubris if it put him (as his remote relative Harry King had, several times), some of the point might have been shed. However image it this way: On Bart's initial pass down the road in the falling short afternoon sun, your house looks peaceful and deserted, without cars and truck in the driveway and also the white Christmas-tree bulbs through chintz curtains the only interior lights he can see. So he parks around the corner, straightens his gas-company uniform, as well as walks up to your home, as bold as brass.

There's a strange, threadbare top quality Bart can notice, he attempted to describe to Billy, even on the front patio. The fading paint, the suet hanging in a rusting wire basket for the cold birds, the aging wood of the home window frames -- they need to have informed him something, must have cautioned him. Yet the lock on the front door is a gallery item, nearly an insult to a contemporary thief educated up on digital alarms, as well as a couple of secs with his picks is all he needs to please it open and also slip within.

Threadbare. It's one of those words that's virtually a tale, all on its own. The wingback chairs, the patterned rugs on the timber flooring, also the parson's table in the entryway, loaded with knickknacks and relatively created to journey a reckless thief-- they're all a little used or torn: not run down, specifically, or dirty; well took care of, in fact. However they recommend, in some way, that they've seen better days. That the world itself, possibly, has seen far better days.

Peering meticulously nearby, Bart spies in the sitting room a Xmas tree straight out of an old publication advertisement. You know the kind: pewter and glass accessories dangling down. The fat bulbs of old- made white lights, swirled like soft ice-cream cones, clipped on the branches. A bright star ahead. As well as there, among the touch of little presents on the red skirt around the base of the tree, waits a white box with an intense gold bow.

As he approaches the tree, Bart discovers himself inching previous yet one more crowded table, this set overruning with a crèche: shepherds, Wise Males, the Holy Family members-- joined by a charge of little wooden, stone, china, and also metal animals. It's as though the remnants of a dozen old Noah's Ark sets had actually made a decision, simultaneously, to go and stare upon the Baby Jesus.

Elephants, camels, giraffes, horses, raccoons, and porcupines. Wildebeests, wolverines, and also wombats, for all that Bart could inform. The mass migration filled the table, while from the high cliff top of a neighboring upright piano, a second wave of the menagerie looked down in marvel.

" They are rather a jumble, aren't they?" pipelines a little voice from throughout the room, freezing Bart in place. "But each of them was a gift from a student, and also how can I have Christmas without establishing them out? I'm sorry. I have to have nodded off right here, waiting. Oh, Johnny, what took you as long?"

III

Ninety, she must be, Bart told Billy. Ninety, ninety-five, a hundred, who could claim? Old, anyhow, and white haired, a small figure snuggled in an upholstered chair throughout the space, with a discolored tartan throw rug curtained over her.

" Forgive me," she includes. "I'm always a little at 6s as well as 7s when I awaken, nowadays. You're not Johnny, naturally. Come assist me up, dear, and we'll place on some tea."

Therefore, in a kind of daze, master thief Bart Sagan strings his way across the room and also reduces Cicely D'Angelo, as vulnerable as a winter months bird, up from her chair and also into the kitchen area.

" There we are," she begins to prattle. "Now, let me place on the water, and if you would not mind, the mugs and also saucers are in the hall, because awful old closet of my mommy's. It's foolish of me, I recognize, to keep the impressive point, with the house currently crowded. But my mother was so happy with it.

Bear in mind? She had it in the shop, where every site visitor might see it, there in your home on Stilton Method when I was a girl."

She turns and also smiles at Bart. "No, just how silly of me. Obviously you do not remember that house. You really should forgive me my rambling. A strong boy like you: You're also busy to understand, normally. However at some point, when life slows down, you'll find the previous survives mainly in old points. Old things and also the memories they hold. Closets, pieces of precious jewelry, those Christmas pets: Every one of them has a story it wishes to tell. A story it does tell, a lot of days. Chatter, babble, babble. I tell you, some days I think I will freak, your home is so full of noise."

Bart nods as well as steps toward the front of your house. He plans, naturally -- naturally, he stopped his story to point out words to Billy: a few moments caught with the old woman, and he's currently saying points like normally-- to glide right out the front door. However then Cicely calls out, "Don't neglect the creamer and the sugar dish, dear. We'll use the porcelain my sister Amelia repainted, with all those foolish little flowers on them.

Anemone, asphodels, and also China asters, if you can think it."

That makes Bart quit to look through the top glass doors of the cupboard at the sets of recipes, as well as before he quite understands why, he's choosing the items of the delicate tea set and also shuttling them to the cooking area. "Leave the teapot below, dear, and also prepare the hinge on the tiny table in the front room, if you would certainly be so kind. Paper napkins in the dining-room sideboard," Cicely adds kindly.

Certainly, then he needs to make an added trip to the dining room for the silver. A journey to the cooking area for a platter of cookies and also the hot teapot. Yet another trek to the hall for the plates he had actually failed to remember on his very first visit, and by the time every little thing is prepared and Cicely is set down on her needlepoint chair to pour the tea, Bart has started to really feel that possibly he truly can make use of a treat.

" Star-of-Bethlehem, that's for satisfaction, isn't it?" asks Cicely, while Bart tries manfully to obtain an actual ingest from his fragile cup. "A pink increased stands for poise. Early morning magnificences indicate 'I love fruitless.' Do you understand the language of flowers, dear? Our mother taught it to us when we were young, yet I can't rather remember what these painted flowers of Amelia's are meant to be stating. Something sad as well as heartfelt, no doubt. Amelia took such delight in being moody. What an elegance she was, the boys swirling around her. However she always danced away, a tragic smile on her face as though they had damaged her heart-- as opposed to vice versa."

She gazes down at the tea table up until finally she whisperings, "There's rosemary, that's for remembrance. Hope you, like, bear in mind. And also there is pansies, that's for ideas. Shakespeare recognized the language of flowers, obviously. There's a sissy. I would certainly give you some violets, however they withered all when my father died. Oh, Johnny, do you keep in mind those purple lilacs you brought, the first time you came calling? So sickly sweet, a boy's dream of what blossoms need to be. I assumed they were for Amelia, however no, my papa claimed, a young man had actually brought them for me."

She closes her eyes for enough time that Bart starts to make his retreat, picturing she's gone to sleep. But his teacup rattles as he sets it down, as well as Cicely returns from her memories. "All done, dear?" she asks. "Aid me clear these dishes away, after that, and also you can inform me why you've come."

The amusing point is, he's attracted to tell her the truth. Oh, while they're cleaning up-- Cicely cleaning at the sink, Bart drying close to her-- he checks out his story of being simply a guy from the gas business, quiting to read the meter. But Cicely simply responds to, "Are you, dear? That seems unlikely," and sends him back to the dining room to do away with the silver.

As well as by the time they're cleared up companionably in the front room, Bart has fallen into a kind of questioning resignation, fiddling with a little bowl of grains on a side table and also waiting to see what comes to pass.

" I can not believe how many years I've saved those. Glass grains, absolutely nothing fancy, naturally, yet, oh, I felt so fine wearing them. A boy named Johnny was pertaining to take me to a sphere at the college, and also my sister Amelia headed out as well as got me a pendant to wear. We drove in a taxi-- my initial taxi flight with anyone other than my dad-- and we danced and also danced. Such dances, and also he kissed me. However the pendant damaged, and also those loose grains in the bowl are all I can take. I still remember how they looked, glimmering there on the polished wood flooring of the ballroom. It was simply an affordable little thing, but I often assume I've invested the rest of my life searching for the lost items.".

She grins as well as satisfies Bart's eyes across the table. "And you, dear?

What are you looking for? I can inform, you recognize. There's something you're contemplating, there in your heart.".

So, almost in a desire, Bart tells her. Tells the white-haired, bright-eyed Cicely D'Angelo the entire thing: the tale of Billy, the accident-prone medication jogger, and also the tale of Harry King, the harsh emperor, making a play for respectability even while he taxed the community's offenders. The undependable brains of Liz McCally, attracted into the plot when she fooled the shipping business for the mailing list. Her worrisome relative, the doob Joey Jasper, avoiding to Minnesota to fetch a far-off package. Also the burglary he had actually committed that mid-day, lifting three kilos of heroin from close to a stack of clinical costs in the pantry of Michael Stuyvesant's empty estate-- Bart clarifies all of it.

" Why would you do that?" Billy disrupted to ask when Bart reached this point in his tale. "I suggest, that's crazy. I do not get it. I don't obtain it, at all.".

" I understand, Billy," he addressed. "Yet that's why I'm informing you all this-- because you haven't been getting it. And also the time has actually come for you to begin.".

After Bart completes defining the globe closing know him like a vise, Cicely responds and says, "It's a puzzle, isn't it? Place on some music, over there in the edge, while I correct the alignment of a little and also see if I can not think about some suggestions for you." She battles up and also includes, "The difficulty is actually your good friends, isn't it? Holding them risk-free? Yes, we need to locate some way for you to keep watch over your group. And that uncomfortable young man who shed the plans, as well. He's come into your life, the poor sheep, and also currently you have to take care of him, too.".

So while Cicely putters among the bric-a-brac in the front room, each of the pets in the crèche's long procession receiving a dusting, Bart takes a look at the records on the racks close to the ancient Victrola in the edge.

-- a stand-alone phonograph gamer, built in a refined wood cabinet. The Andrews Sisters and Vic Damone are there. Dinah Coast. Perry Como bellowing "Some Enchanted Evening," and also Nat King Cole feeling his method with "Nature Boy": The greatest point you'll ever learn,/ Is just to enjoy as well as be enjoyed in return. Peggy Lee, Bing Crosby, the Mills Brothers-- a twisting via two decades of popular music. Taking out a Christmas cd almost at random, Bart slides the record from its paper sleeve as well as establishes it thoroughly on the turntable, the songs rising just over the reduced hum of televisions warming up in the old equipment.

" That's lovely, dear," Cicely calls. "Now come assistance me dirt while we placed our heads with each other. My father was an attorney, you understand, and I remember a few of the mobsters that would certainly concern consult with him. So rushing, my sibling and I thought them, in their fashionable fits as well as hats. Yet not constantly the brightest of men. Intelligent in their own method, no doubt, with an eye on the primary opportunity, yet no, not awfully good thinkers.".

Bart close to her, straightening out the crèche, she adds, "And that's your trouble, isn't it, dear? Oh, you're one of the sharp ones, I can see. However it's insufficient to be clever. You additionally have to be smart." She stops briefly, and also behind-the-scenes, Bart might listen to the soft vocal singing of a carol, Birthing presents we pass through afar. "Not every person has that opportunity, you understand. Up on the piano, towards the front, do you see a pair of elephants? Sculpted from some African tree, I believe. Among my students gave them to me-- sent them from overseas for Xmas, long after I 'd showed him in institution. Such a charming kid.".

She researches the little wooden pets Bart has actually climbed to remove for her. "Yes, a lovely young boy. Gone currently, of course," she sighs. "Every couple of years, while I was instructing, I would have one of you in my class, you know. Bright boys yet remote, their eyes always focused off coming up as though they were looking for something to lead them. As though they were watching for a sign.".

" Ah, well," Cicely adds, her voice tiring. "Set these back on the piano, dear, and allow's coating here. They say elephants never forget, and possibly that's my issue-- not neglecting. I desire I might tell you what to do, yet one really feels one is not really enabled, nowadays. Except maybe for this: Attempt to be wise. All you brilliant young children, so smart and wonderful-- you require to find out to believe not only exactly how but also why. Yes, don't be afraid to puzzle it through, locating what it absolutely indicates. As well as along the way, see if you can't locate a various star to follow. Your gifts were given you for better things than this." She raids Bart and also whisperings in fatigue, "Oh, as well as wed the woman, dear. There will be time enough to be alone. Time enough, Lord knows.".

As Bart overviews her back across the crowded area to her chair, Cicely begins to guide in time with the last song on the document, a melody he can't fairly bear in mind from the far-off side of youth. "Oh, Johnny," she whispers, "I recognized you would return to dance with me again. Why did you steer clear of so long?" As well as there in the last stress of the soft songs, he kisses her hair and also covers her carefully with the blanket as she sleeps once again, as light as snow.

An action throughout the room to switch off the Victrola, a reluctant stop to stoop down, getting rid of the bag of medications from the box beneath the tree, and also Bart stops briefly in the entrance to recall at her. "I desire I might have been Johnny for you," he says quietly. "I wish he had returned.".

" I understand, dear," Cicely D'Angelo surprises him with a last answering murmur. "Yet Johnny was lost in the war, ages ago. Ages and ages earlier. Be well, my love. Be smart.".

IV.

Even at the very early afternoon hr when the gray city skies was as light as December would certainly enable it and also a lot of the town had completed lunch, each as each could, in accordance with the cash they possessed, or can obtain or steal-- also right now when the crosswalks teemed with harried salespersons tardily rushing back to work as well as money males walking smoothly in their opulent topcoats to what they guaranteed each other were their essential professions, while swarms of Christmas customers, the season's yearly visitors, having actually removed bare the shelves and also display cases of the midtown stores, lined the curbs and also groaned for taxis-- even, for that matter, while the wonderful bells in the drab downtown churches rested after their noontime peals and also collected toughness for the Arrival night's Angelus, and also the loud taxis barked by unstopping, indifferent to the sidewalks thick with shivering people screaming into their cell phones, and the Salvation Army's Santas furiously sounding hand bells over their red donation kettles, as well as the distressed delivery trucks beeping in a discordant choir as they tried to back right into filling areas, like some psycho's electronic effort to render "The Carol of the Bells" in one of the most pointless and profane tones he might locate; basically, also as all the noticeable world had actually come to be a busy Xmas cityscape right out of a Charles Dickens story-- even then, Bart Sagan rested unmoving on the home window seat and also stared out at the snowy, busy scene listed below him 3 days he had remained there inside his apartment, overlooking the progressively agitated telephone call as well as poundings at the door. 3 days with absolutely nothing obtained given that he had taken the bundles from Michael Stuyvesant and also Cicely D'Angelo, with Harry King's target date-- and the possibility that the white and also gold present boxes would certainly be opened up at Xmas-- falling down on him like an avalanche.

Not that the days had actually been completely thrown away, although Bart wouldn't understand that till lastly, at an early stage December 23rd, the 4th early morning since his break-ins started, he mixed himself-- bundling up and also going out into the chilly to start job. As well as it was down on the edge of State and Main, within sight of Harry King's building, that Bart saw Toby Veck and his daughter Meg, scam artist with whom he as well as Liz sometimes worked, cleaning past the hardcase stick-up male Caleb Plummer and also providing him the wink.

Interested to see what can bring the dissimilar crooks together, Bart showed up his collar, took down his hat, as well as resolved right into a mindful shadow, following them up State Street towards the sanctuary. Following them, in fact, till they pertained to a modern-looking apartment building, among the addresses

-- simply to be sure, Bart ducked behind a Santa and reindeer display as well as inspected his duplicate of the list-- to which a heroin bundle had been sent.

In itself, that was enough of a coincidence to set Bart stressing. Yet after that he saw Meg and Caleb take up the areas of yet more criminals he recognized: the pickpocket May Fielding as well as the safecracker Will certainly Fern, that

casually slipped Toby their notebooks as well as strolled off arm in arm, approximating as finest they might an innocent set of Xmas shoppers. Toby responded to his little girl and the armed burglar, filched the previous viewers' notebooks, and also walked off himself, transforming east on Third.

It took Bart a number of hours to piece together the operation, and he located himself inordinately happy that he had lost the skeptical Toby just as soon as-- when, after making a call from a pay phone, the old guy had actually suddenly marched into the road to hail a taxi and speed up off, while Bart suggested vainly with a lady, her arms full of Christmas bundles, who claimed the taxi he had desperately handled to quit. However Bart picked up Toby again when, finding at last another taxicab, he made a hunch and also routed the driver to the closest unvisited address on the delivery company's checklist.

By the time Toby switched on High Street, hunching his shoulders versus the wind, and disappeared right into the Evergreen Tavern, Bart had actually seen him make five quits-- visiting, like a police officer's negative desire, as strange a collection of the city's offenders as anyone could envision. Teacher Redlaw, the bilker, and also the hulking Tetterby siblings (although Bart was sure he would certainly heard they were still behind bars for every little thing from tried murder to intensified jaywalking). The get-away chauffeurs Milly as well as Expense Swidger. The pencil-thin fence Ben Britain, of all people, and Clemency Newcome, that had chosen long back never ever to meet the name with which her confident parents had baptized her. Also blonde as well as blue-eyed Michael Warden, the widows' buddy, of whom the very best that might be claimed was that he may not rob an orphanage if he already had some cash in his pocket.

Bart hesitated a surprisingly long period of time in the vestibule of a made use of- clothing store down the street, acting to take a look at the window screen of dated connections, dusty outfit precious jewelry, and the remains of last summer's flies-- an economical glass necklace blinking at him in the angled morning light. It had not been be afraid that made him stop briefly, he determined. It was much more a desire not to recognize, not to be attracted right into, whatever his friends as well as service associates had obtained themselves as much as. He currently lacked a plan for deflecting Harry King's hazards against the community's minor offenders, as well as below were those very same bad guys running around in some crazy effort to make points extra challenging.

Yet he understood, naturally, that he had to deal with up to it, and so at last, with a sigh, his hand on his hat to keep it from surprising, Bart walked up the block and also opened the tavern door-- just to be hit by a wave of noise thatnearly knocked him back out once again into High Street.

There was Gruff Tackleton, a gigantic goat of a guy, screaming across the space while he maintained watch on the door. Snitchy and Craggs. Arthur Heathfield. Dr. Jeddler, the sometime doctor, that would certainly fix up a bullet injury if he was sober enough to see it. Sitting at bench, having taken over the daily-specials chalkboard, was Bart's accountant, the elfin Mr. Filer, preparer of deceptive income tax return for most of town's abyss. Nobody knew his given name, and tale had it that he never left his office-- sleeping on the sofa and food preparation his little meals on a hot plate out of anxiety the IRS would certainly slip in and bug the location while he was gone. Yet below he was at the Evergreen, marking down times as well as areas in yellow chalk.

" Bart!" shouted Dot Perrybingle from the table where she sat with her slow, lumbering sibling John, as well as like a wave in an arena words spread throughout the tavern. Mad Tilly, tying tiny, precise knots in a piece of string. Hazardous Joe Bowley. The party ladies and also periodic intruders Poise as well as Marion. Thieves and grifters and also prowlers; pickpockets, crooks, and also scroungers; burglars, heisters, and also hijackers. Every person from highway robbers to shoplifters seemed to be gathered, a larcenous setting up of the community's crooks. And perched there at the center, as pleased as a catbird, was his buddy Liz McCally.

" Oh, Bart," she wept. "What took you so long?"

" A Tom and Jerry for every of you," Tim the bartender revealed, putting down a set of frothing Christmas cups, red with white snows, as Bart sat at Liz's table with all the calm confidence of a guy that suspects his chair is wired with dynamites and also intends to shoot the people accountable. "Dance Dan brought in his special recipe. Everybody here has actually been consuming them, the past few days, while they have actually been ... "-- he flinched far from Liz's glare--" doing whatever it is they have actually been doing. I don't ask concerns." Averting and also striding throughout the room, he added in a loud voice, "Hey, men, can you maintain it down to a boring roar? The sweeties require to chat."

Bart looked down at his warm beverage, sprinkled with cinnamon. He gazed up at the Christmas decors and gazed over at the crowded bar. He transformed his head sidewards to check out the notebooks where Liz had been keying information into her laptop. He even swiveled to research the tables to the left, to the right, ahead, at his back, as well as only then-- as the noise of bench gradually reduced-- did he meet the eyes of the pretty, apprehensive face across the table as well as ask, in the most reasonable tone he could take care of, "What in God's name have you done, Liz?"

" It ... well, it got a little unmanageable, perhaps," she answered. "However truly," she added, acquiring rate, "all this is your fault. Okay, I made some telephone call, and also everybody I talked to wanted to lend a hand. And then they made call, as well as, yeah, the people they called made more call, and also by the end of the opening night I had more assistance than I recognized what to do with, and also the word was still spreading. You disappeared for days, my relative Joey called me from Minnesota yelling for recommendations about the job you sent him on, and nobody has an idea how to stop Harry King. So what was I intended to do?"

She was sputtering by this point, her stress and anxiety having actually altered by some strange alchemy into rage. "Days," Liz duplicated. "Days, without a word. Days, without telling me what I must be doing. So, I. I," she failed, glimpsing about as well as discovering as if for the very first time just how complete the pub had come to be. "I presume I sort of organized points."

But as Bart opened his mouth to speak, she started up once again. "Anyhow, what right do you need to slam? If you can't be liable, Bart, then someone else has to be. Besides"-- and also her tone expanded even more wheedling--" we have actually currently located where all the plans are. And also I've chatted two of our close friends into flying out and aiding Joey, but that was mainly since I didn't know what to do with them, as well as they said they needed to lie reduced for some time."

She held up a finger to quit Bart from disrupting while she gulped at her drink. "There's lots more," she included a rush. "We've got every local location under security, with notes regarding the locals and security system and also plans, where we might find them, every little thing written down.

Plus Harry King's area. Billy Euston has been helping with that. You bear in mind: King's nephew in-law or something, the man that lost the medications. He came in right here recently, trying to find you, so I placed him to function. Mr.

Filer has actually been maintaining the watch routines, and Professor Redlaw tricked a clerk down at city hall for drain maps, in case we require them, as well as everyone has been joining in, despite the fact that it's Christmastime."

Liz took an additional ingest. "However finding the packages, that's the important point. As well as I took care of to maintain everyone in check, just like you stated—even though they were all pressing me to begin swapping out the medications. Oh, as well as we've bought some good white wine, a set of containers weighing exactly enough. Afterwards, I wished to send them home, however I couldn't, because it's, like, Xmas with each other, you understand? Everybody was being so useful, and also we were interacting as a group, as well as you were missing out on, and also I really did not have a plan. They all want some means to pull Harry King down, yet nobody can determine anything except to obtain the plans as well as offer him what he wants, as well as it's driving them insane. Crazy," she said with a choking laugh. "Crazy.".

" They despise King that a lot?" asked Bart, ultimately getting in a word. "You idiot," she screamed, the entire tavern dropping silent and counting on appearance. "They didn't concern obtain Harry King. They concerned aid you.".

" The length of time given that you rested?" Bart asked Liz gently in the following silence.

" I do not understand. A couple days. Things simply type of grown out of control, as well as I had to go on top of them. I suggest, it's December 23rd currently, and also we have actually obtained absolutely nothing.".

" No," Bart answered. "I took care of to raise two of the bundles, the ones out in the suburban areas. So you can call off your watchers there. For the rest, what do we have? Timetables of shipments? A checklist of the various locks? Notes on that has gain access to?".

" Whatever," Liz responded, sitting up as she saw Bart check out the space as though considering up the toughness and also weak points surrounding them. "We have every little thing any person could find out over 3 days, which"-- she gestured down at the heap of note pads--" ends up being a lot.".

Bart glimpsed around the room again. "You don't even like half these people, Liz," he claimed silently.

" Yeah, well, they're offenders. What do you expect? However they're all their own crooks, if that makes any feeling. They aren't sneaks, and they don't come from Harry King. Well, other than possibly for Billy Euston. I can not identify what he's doing below, day in day out, moping about, waiting on you like you're some kind of expert that's mosting likely to fill him with old wisdom. However all I've said is that we're servicing what his manager demanded, so what else can he report back to King? I imply, that is what we're doing, isn't it? Obeying Harry King's orders? Unless you've obtained a strategy I don't recognize around.".

But Bart didn't answer, evaluating instead at the unpleasant youngster hunched in the edge-- truly looking, seeing for the very first time his sadness and bitterness, his hunger for something much more. After that Bart's fingers began to move on the table, nearly as though he were playing subconscious ranges on an unseen piano, and he elevated his eyes to focus for a lengthy minute on some remote horizon.

" Bart?" Liz called. "Bart? BART? Are you listening?" "Hmm?" he addressed, returning to her.

" I asked if you have a plan.".

He satisfied her eyes as well as grinned for the very first time in days. "I believe I might, sweetheart. I believe I simply might.".

Bart took an ingest from his Tom as well as Jerry. "You know, Tim was right," he stated, like a food doubter taking some time from a busy schedule to appreciate a tidbit. "These are good. Not a breakfast drink specifically, yet we need to obtain Dan's recipe.".

" As God is my witness," the red-eyed Liz hissed, "if you don't tell me, I'm going to shoot you as well as have every person right here indicate it was understandable homicide.".

" I can't discuss all of it. Not yet. Allow me maintain one shock, just in case points go bad," Bart clarified. "However here's exactly how it starts. I require to have a talk with Billy. Maybe do a little searching for products today. After that we'll strike every one of the continuing to be places either this afternoon or tonight. Nine tasks straight. This is mosting likely to be impressive.".

He pulled over among the notebooks, tore out a sheet, and began taking down notes. "In the meanwhile, I need you to put together a schedule for the hits. Which ones in daylight? Which ones at night? Cons or sneak-ins? No strong-arm if you can help it, but one way or another, they all have to be done long prior to daybreak. By twelve o'clock at night, if we potentially can.".

He highlighted something on the web page. "Obtain a few individuals to assist you lay it out. Redlaw, perhaps. And Mr. Filer, since he's here. Meg Veck, also: Time for her to discover just how to tip up, whatever her father states.".

He studied his notes for a moment and also included, "You'll need among the real thiefs know the preparation, also. Heathfield, I think; he's the best of them. Appoint a hard-case or 2 to every job as back-up and defense, yet don't allow them take the lead. We desire these to go quietly. Make Gruff Tackleton component of your inner team as well as use him to maintain the tough guys in line; he's a pro and knows just how it works.".

Bart made one last note, circled something, as well as chuckled as he looked down at the paper. "And also there we are. Establish the tasks so I can join as numerous as possible, one after one more." He laughed once again, going back to the high-energy Bart that Liz had actually always understood prior to. "A kind of rolling hit. A Xmas criminal offense spree. Take a look at it in this manner, Liz: We're mosting likely to do a reverse Santa Claus -- taking something from every person on our list, whether they've been mischievous or nice.".

He stood up and also called across the tavern, "Billy, will you take a walk with me outside? I have actually obtained a story I intend to inform you." Then he turned back to the table and took a final swallow from his drink. "You understand," he duplicated in a questioning tone. "These are really excellent. I'll call you by midday, one o'clock at the current, and inform you if it's on for today.".

Then Bart Sagan, the thief, leaned down as well as kissed Liz McCally the grifter on the leading her head. "Many thanks, sweetie, for everything. You've conserved all of us," he whispered. And also in a swirl of activity, he made his way across the room-- smiling, touching shoulders, greeting the town's bad guys. Gathering the battered drug-runner Billy Euston and purging the door into the chilly wind of High Road.

V.

It ends ... however after that, these kinds of stories do not finish. Not actually. They only flicker every now and then with small surprises and revelations, like the dropping of a curtain across the stage to indicate a break: the conclusion of one certain act in the lengthy human funny.

Consider it as the verdict of a chapter as opposed to the closing of a publication. The affluent but sick Michael Stuyvesant, for instance-- where will his curtain fall? The panic-stricken Joey Jasper, off in Minnesota, for that issue? And Harry King, the drug lord, and that obsequious jewelry expert that sold him a half-million-dollar necklace for his spouse, sliding like starlight with Mr.

King's thick hands? Cicely D'Angelo, dreaming in her chair. The bruiser Gruff Tackleton. The sneak-thieves Snitchy and also Craggs. Everybody has a various phase. Every person comes to a various end.

Yet given that this is Bart's tale, basically, we need to most likely leave the tale where he set it down-- on a table at the Evergreen Tavern on.

Xmas Eve, covered neatly in red paper with a white bow: a tiny Christmas present, waiting for Liz McCally to get here.

Naturally, to get to that point, the community's wrongdoers had to obtain 9 of the twelve packages in a single day, and also the rolling Christmas criminal offenses began just around one in the afternoon, when Bart ultimately telephoned to inform Liz the campaign got on.

The information are still a little unclear. Every person concurs that, in the rush, Mr. Filer became the point guy: the little accountant in a rigid dark fit, balanced on a bar feces as he tracked the jobs, swiftly coming to be the only one with the entire image. However considering that he was also the kind of male that would not tell a nun whether it was drizzling-- wouldn't tell her mom superior and a choir of angels, as far as that goes-- no one has actually ever heard his account of the day's events. Bart stayed in the field, Liz was too impatient not to hurry out to join him, and everybody else had only a partial view of how things unfolded. The Evergreen's bartender Tim sometimes talks about it, gassing away to regulars on a slow night, however it's hard to state what components of his variation are myth, layered on like icing, as well as what parts actually took place.

Anyway, as the tale goes, only one of the jobs broke down right into the kind of strong-arm break-in that both Bart as well as Mr. King intended to prevent. The drugs were being held, for an out-of-town tenant, behind the concierge workdesk of an upscale and also remarkably scam-proof apartment building. After two fell short disadvantages (a postman gag and then an impromptu try by Liz, spilling points from her bag while she requested instructions), the Tetterby siblings had had sufficient. With a growl, they squeezed out of the watchers' vehicle, marched in, banged the officious staff down versus the desk when he objected, got the Xmas box, as well as marched out again-- a single Tetterby finger, pointed menacingly, enough to freeze in position every person else in the structure's lobby.

That was one of the drug packages that really did not get replaced with Liz's wine bottles. Other addresses, nevertheless, confirmed much more open. Two, as an example, were straight-forward daytime slip-ins-- a peaceful picking of backdoor locks while your houses' homeowners were out. Discover the boxes (one under a tree, the various other unwrapped on an entry table), make the substitutions, and relock the doors: in and out, as graceful as dancers. Will Certainly Fern and also May Fielding paired for those tasks.

Professor Redlaw's graphes of the storm-sewer lines never ever did get utilized.

There seems to have been a plan to follow them to an accessibility hatch in the basement of an additional apartment building, yet when the break-in team showed up, they found a fire door that hadn't fairly latched and determined they might also maintain their clothes clean.

Regrettably, once inside, they located the white Xmas box not only unpacked however opened: the tape-wrapped bag of medications remaining on the cooking area counter with a yellow sticky note that checked out, "Bob-- Is this intended to be some type of joke?" After a collection of significantly acrimonious phone calls, the drunk Dr. Jeddler developed the answer, yelling it throughout the pub to Mr. Filer. So Dot Perrybingle and her brother John very carefully slit the bundle, emptied its heroin right into a trash can, and also replenished it with flour, sugar, as well as cooking soda they borrowed from the cabinets. A little wiping up and hiding of the evidence, some re-taping of the plan, as well as the Perrybingles left the house pretty much as they had actually located it-- minus, naturally, the heroin, an environment-friendly plastic trash bag, and also 6.6 extra pounds of cooking products.

As for the swaps accomplished by the con artists, the initial was in a house with a for-sale sign in the snow on the front lawn. A check out to the real estate professional by Poise as well as the handsome Michael Warden cracked that open as very easy an egg. Joe Bowley as well as the grim Clemency Newcome took the two in run- down houses down by the river-- impersonating city inspectors on a search for violations and bulldozing the building supervisors into a cooperative mindset. The most significant scam involved a phony city-services team, a genuine gas leak that began to leave control, as well as a 911 phone call that brought three fire engine, 2 police wagons, and an ambulance shouting up the icy streets. A half-dozen scam artist it required to develop that little masterpiece of overkill, leaving three homes evacuated and also two fistfights started prior to they ultimately handled to escape with the medicines.

And after that there was the last task: a good, antique, not-a-creature-was-stirring burglary, the household asleep in their beds. Bart as well as Arthur Heathfield took that. As Tim informs the tale, a little lady captured them, cushioning down the stairways in her nightgown to ask what they were doing under the tree. To which, naturally, they answered that they were Santa's helpers, offered her a glass of milk, and sent her back up the staircases to bed. However not even the pub's regulars truly think him. Some stories are way too much like stories to be true.

Still, this much is particular: It was after midnight-- a couple of minutes into Xmas Eve Day-- that Bart climbed to say thanks to the offenders reconvened at the Evergreen. One eco-friendly trash can as well as 10 clear plastic plans of heroin secure in a traveling bag in the trunk of his car, as well as nine jobs carried out in a solitary day: a brave, nearly amazing endeavor.

" Marion," he asked, getting to down as well as carefully tugging from Mad Tilly's cool fingers the item of origami she was folding from one of the stray note pads pages, "will you as well as Mr. Filer make sure all this paper gets shed or shredded? As for the rest of you, if you visit after 5:00 in the afternoon, there will be Xmas provides right here for everybody." Liz made a noise to disrupt, however Bart bypassed her. "I know, I recognize. None of you did this for pay. But I'm grateful-- happy past words-- so allow me attempt to share my appreciation with a thank-you gift.".

"Man, these are good," he added, sipping at his last Tom and Jerry of the day. "Dan, send me the recipe, and I swear I'll add a little extra, just for you." He put a hand on Tilly's shoulder and said, "Meanwhile, I've got one or two more jobs to do tonight. Some presents to fix up. Tilly, you're good at wrapping things. Will you help me? Everyone else, thank you again. Thank you."

Gesturing to Billy Euston to join them, Bart shrugged into his overcoat and made his way to the door. "Oh, and one last thing," he called back. "Sleep in tomorrow, Liz. You've done enough for all of us."

And while the criminals cheered her, Bart and his companions left the warm tavern and ventured out in the cold Christmas Eve morning, following the illumination of a distant streetlight to his car.

"Did you hear the news?" the bartender Tim called out as Liz came through the door of the Evergreen Tavern on Christmas Eve, a little before 5:00 in the afternoon.

"No," she answered with a smile. "What news? I haven't heard a thing." In fact, Liz had slept late—very late—that morning, reveling in what seemed her first peaceful rest in ages. And then, resolutely refusing to check her messages or answer her phone, she'd spent the remainder of the day in a happy haze: puttering around her apartment, doing small chores, wrapping presents, humming softly to herself.

"Oh, nothing much," Tim said, in his element as purveyor of drinks and the latest word. "Just that Bart is on the run, Harry King is in jail, the police chief is on a rampage, and half the town has gone crazy. Gunfights, I hear, down by the river. Some Yuletide we're having, isn't it?"

"Bart's on the run?" Liz repeated bewilderedly. "Wait, what are you talking about? I don't . . . I mean . . . King's in jail? Where's Bart?"

"That's what I'm trying to tell you," said Tim, and, in his account, it all begins earlier that day, when Harry King gives his wife a present in front of his guests at an afternoon Christmas reception. Rich food, a string quartet, an open bar, unctuous speeches about King's past innocence but future promises not to sully himself "by association with those less concerned" than King "with a moral appearance and the city's good name." And then the gift giving, starting with the announcement of a large charitable donation to the city's cultural foundations and ending with a present for King's wife.

Which she unwraps, to the continuation of general applause, and reveals as a velvet-covered jewelry case. A jewelry case, as it happens, that looks as though it's leaking dust. And when she snaps it open on its spring hinges, it jumps in her hands, spraying fine white powder over the women next to her—one of them the city council's representative for district three. It's in their hair, down their cleavage, on their hands: a mess that makes them look like the powdered ghosts of eighteenth-century French courtiers, come back as the revenge of Louis XIV.

Well, the string quartet falls silent, the guests freeze, Harry King is ready to explode, and nobody knows what to do. Nobody, that is, but the district attorney's recent bride—beautiful, greedy, and empty-headed beyond even the town's usual standard for rich men's third wives—who has taken the opportunity to tear open the neat wrapping of her own gift box.

"Oh," she cries into the silence, and every head turns toward her. "What are we supposed to use this for? Is it expensive?"

Very expensive, as things turn out, for what she's holding up in her pretty hands for all to see is a taped-up plastic package, filled with white powder and weighing, at a guess, around 6.6 pounds.

Now others in the room start opening their boxes to find similar gifts. The white-powdered councilwoman meets the eye of a senior police official, who nods and uses his pocket knife to cut a small hole in his own package. Touching a tiny portion to his tongue, he spits and starts beckoning wildly for his aide, the young policeman who accompanied him to the party.

And that was pretty much that. Oh, there were still scenes to be played out: Harry King's bellowing, and his own associates' deciding maybe discretion was the better choice, quietly wiping their fingerprints off their guns and hiding them in napkins as the police came charging through the door. Paramedics summoned to keep the heroin-dusted women from getting drug poisoning. Loud demands from the mayor to be told what was going on.

But really, everything was determined, the whole drama moving toward its predictable end, from the moment Mrs. King opened the case of what was supposed to be a diamond necklace from her husband. As the police took statements and gathered evidence, Harry King, lord of all he could see, was led from the room in handcuffs. Not, however, before having a whispered but heated conference with his lawyer, in which—rumor among the town's criminals insisted—the name of Bart Sagan was repeated several times.

Liz McCally lowered herself slowly onto the seat of a back booth—the same booth in which had she sat, only six days before, to hear the story of Billy Euston's blunder and Harry King's threats. Bart had come by the tavern, oh, must have been around 1:00, the bartender had said, leaving some things for her and promising to call just after 5:00.

What she found in the booth were a set of thick white envelopes, two dozen or so, lined up between the salt and pepper shakers. Baskets on the opposite bench overflowing like Santa's bag with jars of caviar and truffles—Sumatran coffee at $600 a pound and expensive bottles of wine. And there on the table, in front of the spot in which she had sat at their earlier meeting, was a small Christmas package with her name on it, wrapped in red and white.

Avoiding touching the present, avoiding even thinking about it, Liz pulled out one of the envelopes and saw on the front Gruff Tackleton's name in Bart's clear handwriting. Unsealed, of course; he's always too trusting, she thought angrily, deflecting the impulse to cry before it overwhelmed her. Too trusting in too many ways, even while he didn't trust her enough to let her in on the plan to get King—to let *her*, his one real friend, help. Mad Tilly and that stupid kid Billy were the people Bart took with him when he left the Evergreen, the ones who must have been with him when he broke into King's penthouse and planted the drugs.

Inside the envelope she found a half-inch of currency, all hundred-dollar bills: maybe $10,000. Assuming an envelope for everyone who had joined in the jobs the day before, that came to around $250,000. A quarter of a million dollars, just lying there on the table, waiting for Liz to distribute it.

She was finally reaching for the small Christmas present—reaching for it, pulling back as though it had burned her, and then reaching for it again—

when her cell phone rang.

"Hello, Bart," she answered it quietly, at last lifting up the package with her other hand and reading the simple "For Elizabeth Ann McCally" on the label. "Why'd you do it? Why didn't you tell me?"

"I wanted to protect you," he replied in a soothing voice. "King is probably going to be too busy to do much in the way of revenge, but this way, if he does go after anyone, it'll be just me and not you. Not any of the other independents." Bart laughed. "Besides, how's he going to beat a drug rap when he doused some of this city's most respectable people with heroin? I hear they're going to hit him with a dozen charges of attempted murder, on top of possession and trafficking. Meanwhile, every would-be gangster in town is out grabbing a piece of his empire, now that Billy has tipped them off."

"Yeah, Billy," said Liz tonelessly. "Why did you take him with you last night? And poor, crazy Tilly, too?"

"Ah," Bart answered. "You mean, why didn't I take you? I needed Billy to help get me into King's penthouse, guide me through me the layout. And I wanted Tilly because she's the neatest person I know, and we needed to unwrap the presents, pack them with the drugs, and then wrap them again exactly enough that none of King's people would notice they'd been tampered with. I didn't take you because you were exhausted, and because . . . well, because I didn't want you to get caught with me, if something went wrong."

Liz felt her tears starting to rise again and began to open her present as carefully as she could, preserving the paper and bow just to show Bart—or herself, at least—that she was every bit as neat as Tilly. "And all these envelopes?" she asked. "I'm supposed to just hand them out? How can you afford it?"

"Yeah, the envelopes. They cleaned out my emergency get-away fund. Every penny I could lay my hands on, in fact. But I, ah"—Bart laughed again—"I managed to do a little replenishing. You remember when I told you that King said he had to give the bigwigs some quiet money? Well, Billy had overheard the exact amounts. So, while Billy kept watch at the door and Tilly rewrapped the presents, I sat down at King's desk and booted up his computer. Easiest work I've ever done. All I had to do was use the amounts of his last large withdrawals to get online access to his main account."

There was a long crackle of static on the line, as though Bart were going through a tunnel, before he continued, “From there I could reach out to all his other accounts. The Cayman Islands, Europe, here in the city. I cleaned him out, Liz. He kept all his information in that one computer, and I transferred his money to banks scattered around the world. He’s never getting it back. This is a big one, Liz. Even after helping Billy set himself up, it’s enough cash to last me a good long stretch.”

She could almost hear Bart smiling. “By the way,” he added, “did you ever hear any news from Minnesota?”

“Just a message last night from Joey, saying he was still working on it.” Liz had finally peeled off the wrapping paper, revealing a small blue box. “Where are you now?” she asked quietly.

“About a hundred, a hundred and fifty, miles away,” Bart answered. “I figured the airport might be watched, so I’m driving to the coast. Then I thought I’d catch a plane out of the country, till things cool down. Tokyo, maybe, or Singapore. Hong Kong. Out on the Pacific Rim, anyway. You knew I grew up out there, didn’t you? My grandparents were missionaries, and . . . I don’t know, I just started to feel that maybe it was time to go visit for a while. Time to head back to the Far East and get things straight.”

Liz lifted off the top of the box and found under the cotton batting a cheap glass-bead necklace, with a price tag still attached from the used-clothing store a few doors down High Street. “And what’s this?” she asked. “This $12.40 piece of costume jewelry you’ve given me for Christmas?”

“It’s not jewelry, exactly,” he answered, fading as though into the distance. “It’s more like a promise. A promise I’ll come back.” As the cell-phone service dropped the line, replacing Bart Sagan’s voice with a dull buzz, Liz McCally lifted the necklace up to the light, where it danced and glittered against the old, polished wood of the Evergreen Tavern’s ceiling.

And that’s the end of this particular story, the falling of its curtain—except perhaps for one final note. After church on Christmas morning, after the annual phone calls with her great-nieces and nephews, scattered across the country, Cicely D’Angelo laid out for herself in the front room a pot of tea and a plate of cookies from a round blue tin. Perched on her chair, she gazed fondly at the new pairs of animals she had set near her crèche—each of them being greeted, she imagined, by their older companions in the long procession to pay homage to the Holy Infant in a manger. This year’s

Christmas gifts, sent by her young students, of course. Or, rather, not so young. Grown old now themselves, she had to admit, although in memory they still lived as the girls and boys they had been. Such promise, such hope: new lights just beginning to shine.

She dozed off for a moment, or perhaps she merely slipped into her reminiscences, hardly distinguishable from dreams. But returning gently to the waking world, she found her eyes focused on the white box beneath the tree, left by that clever and dangerous young man who had come to visit. The poor child with a terrible puzzle to solve.

Clearing away the tea dishes and washing up, Cicely hummed an old dance tune—not terribly Christmasy, she smiled to think, but that's all right, just this once. Back in the front room, the white box in her lap, she lifted the lid to see whether the thief had left her anything when he slipped out, believing her asleep. And in wonder, from the depths of tissue paper, she brought out a brilliant silver necklace, gems flowing like starlight in her tiny hands. Terribly expensive, it must be, she could see, and much too fine to wear, of course. But then, young men are often foolish that way. Such a lovely boy.

With a sigh, setting the box on the floor, she rose from her chair to set the necklace on the table with her animals, as though it were yet another little gift from yet another student—weaving it carefully around the crèche to lie at the feet of Mary as the Wise Men and shepherds approached the manger. Yes, she decided, that's where it goes: there, among the Christmas things.

www.ingramcontent.com/pod-product-compliance
Lightning Source LLC
LaVergne TN
LVHW040934150826
845672LV00007B/2353

* 9 7 9 8 7 5 8 9 7 6 1 6 6 *